DEDICATION

To learners all across the world who are pursuing a doctorate,
or considering doing so

contact us for more information

COPYRIGHT NOTICE

BluePrint Ambitions
blueprintambitions.com

Copyright © 2022, Dawn McLucas

All rights reserved. Contents of this book may not be reproduced, distributed, or transmitted in any form without the prior written permission of the author.

The information in this book is for general informational and educational purposes. Any advice or recommendations are made without guarantee on the part of the author or publisher. The author and publisher disclaim any liability in connection with the use of this information.

contact us for more information

about the author

MEET DR. DAWN MCLUCAS

Hello future doctors! My name is Dr. Dawn McLucas. I obtained a Bachelor of Science in Business Management, a Master of Business Administration, and a Doctorate of Management in Organizational Leadership. I also have professional experience in training, staffing, disability compensation benefits, and university residential life.

The doctoral journey can be overwhelming. The path to obtain my Doctorate was lengthy and full of ups, down, frustration, and changes. Everyone's journey is different. Only a doctoral student or doctoral graduate can understand and relate to the feelings and experiences encountered during a doctoral program. My experiences and those of fellow doctoral students motivated me to create the Doctorate 101 course and book.

Doctorate 101

MISSION STATEMENT

BluePrint Ambitions

The mission of BluePrint Ambitions is to provide educational and encouraging books and courses that motivate and allow adults to grow, learn, and reach goals.

The purpose of this book is to offer insight, experiences, preparation and encouragement to new and prospective doctoral students. The goal is to allow students to build a skills foundation that can aid in successful and confident progress during a doctoral program. It will offer an introduction to important concepts regarding scholarly writing, best practices, motivation, the dissertation, and oral defense.

Contents

- THE START — 1
- DISSERTATION INTRODUCTION — 2
- GOALS — 3
- EXPECTATIONS — 4

DR. DAWN MCLUCAS

Contents

- POSITIVE FOCUS — 5
- LESSONS LEARNED — 6
- REWARDS — 7
- FINAL THOUGHTS — 8

DR. DAWN MCLUCAS

INTRODUCTION

So, you are thinking about or have decided to pursue your doctorate degree. Let me first congratulate you for deciding to pursue a higher level of education. I know that this is not a decision made lightly. I obtained my Doctor of Management in Organizational Leadership in 2018. I must say, I learned so much about myself along the way. My journey had many more hills and valleys than I anticipated. But in the end, it was definitely worth it. During your doctoral program, you will read and write a significant amount of literature. Therefore, the purpose of this book is to provide a concise summary consisting of experiences, tips, encouragement, and considerations that may benefit and aid you in your doctoral journey. It is an introductory guide on what to expect during the doctoral process.

DOCTORATE 101

1

THE *Start*

Chapter One
THE START

    As I was growing up, I always knew that I planned to go to college to obtain a bachelor's degree. Though I was not always sure of what area I wanted to study. During my senior year of high school, I applied to multiple colleges. After choosing a college, I majored in business management and worked toward a Bachelor of Science in Business Management. Attending college after high school was one of the best decisions I ever made. I greatly enjoyed the freedom of living on campus and getting more real-life experience. I had some fun times and made some lifelong friends. As I moved toward the end of my program, I decided that I wanted to continue my educational endeavors and apply to a master's program.

Chapter One

THE START

I obtained my bachelor's degree and then went straight into a master's program. After I completed the master's program, I began my journey in the real world and started my first post-college job. Life after college was an initial adjustment. However, I did enjoy my introductory positions after college. In the beginning, it didn't cross my mind to continue my education and attempt to obtain a doctorate.

When I began thinking about obtaining my doctorate, I was working full-time in a position that I had held for about a year. I was 2 years post earning my Master's in Business Administration. I consider myself a lifelong learner. I will likely always continue to grow and learn, whether through certifications or classes. I wanted to pursue a Doctorate in Management in order to continue to learn, to possibly teach at the doctoral level, and to achieve higher-level professional positions. At that time, my employer was offering tuition assistance which would pay for most of the cost of the courses. So, I compared schools and decided what format and program would best work for me. I started my doctoral program in 2009.

Chapter One
THE START

 Before choosing a doctoral program, I would encourage you to research schools and curriculums. There are so many different programs available. Furthermore, though different schools offer the same degree, the program and course learning may be different. I would pay close attention to courses offered, degree timeline, and costs. My program consisted of both online courses and in-person residencies. This was the best fit for my life and schedule.

DOCTORATE 101

2

DISSERTATION
Introduction

Chapter Two

DISSERTATION INTRODUCTION

    Each doctorate program is unique and may use various steps and have a range of requirements. As you progress in the program you will encounter choosing a topic, chair and committee assignment, proposal creation, research, and dissertation completion. Some doctoral programs choose your committee members for you. While in other doctoral programs you choose your committee members. The chair is your main committee member and a mentor to help assist in successful completion. The additional committee members also support your progress. Your committee members may be familiar with your chosen topic or research method. In the beginning, you will need to decide on a problem of interest. After choosing this, you will need to decide what type of research design and method you want to use.

    A large component of a doctorate program is the dissertation. A dissertation is the final project you will complete in your program. It is comprised of different sections. The dissertation is a research-themed written document you will complete to address a problem of your choice. In it, you will cover related literature, research, results, and recommendations.

Chapter Two

DISSERTATION INTRODUCTION

Topic

    There are infinite choices for a dissertation topic. It could be related to a problem at your place of employment, an area of interest, or even your program of study. I would encourage you to consider a few different ideas. Then narrow them down. If working on a dissertation related to a current place of employment, I would suggest that you think about your desires regarding staying at your current place of employment or if you are considering changing employers in the near future. If you change employers, will you still have access or permission to complete the research at the former employer? There are numerous considerations to think about.

Chapter Two

DISSERTATION INTRODUCTION

Research Method

The research method chosen can be qualitative or quantitative. In addition, some research projects use both qualitative and qualitative research. Qualitative research strives to examine various views or perspectives. Qualitative research may be done through activities such as interviews or focus groups. Quantitative research focuses on the level at which a change in one variable relates to a change in other variables. Both types of research allow the researcher to gain an understanding and answers regarding the research problem and hypothesis.

For my dissertation, I initially chose quantitative research. However, as I read more and focused on the true purpose of my research study, I changed to qualitative research. It is a good idea to read about different research designs that are available and choose the best fit for your research topic and purpose. There are numerous books available on different research methods and designs. In addition, your school will offer assistance through the articles and books used during coursework.

Chapter Two

DISSERTATION INTRODUCTION
Literature Review

As part of your proposal and dissertation, you may need to complete a literature review. Research has been done on numerous topics over the years. A literature review allows you as the researcher to read historical and more current research studies that have already been completed. The review provides a picture of what has been learned about the topic and what gaps exist. This helps to support the need and purpose for your research study.

The literature review may be one of the most time-consuming portions of your research. The literature review was one of the largest sections of my dissertation. The focus of my dissertation was insurance customer loyalty. I gathered research articles related to different types of insurance and areas of customer loyalty such as retention, satisfaction, and the number of policies held. The search terms that you use to find articles are important. I would recommend starting with broader search terms or comparison searches. Next, I would look for research articles that were done specifically about or very similar to the problem or relationship that you want to explore in your research. This will allow you to see the range of research that has been done.

Chapter Two

DISSERTATION INTRODUCTION

    The main goal is to determine if research for your desired topic is warranted and if there is room for growth that your research can add. You can look through peer-reviewed journals related to your topic. You can also search online for articles to review. The articles reviewed will discuss the related research that was completed, along with the results and recommendations.

    Historical research will need to be examined. Peer-reviewed research articles should be reviewed. The articles will need to be concerning similar areas of your proposed research. The article may have examined the same variables you desire to look at or only parts of the proposed research. It is important to get a grasp of the related historical research, in order to add to the research already completed.

    Current research for the desired topic will also need to be examined. You will need to determine if the current research has solved any problems that historical research found. In addition, the review of more current research findings and recommendations may also assist you in homing in on the problem and hypothesis you want to focus on.

Chapter Two
DISSERTATION INTRODUCTION

Research gaps can be examined after comparing historical research with more current research. Various gaps can be found that will allow you to finalize your research proposal. The review of historical research and current research will help you observe whether the topic has been researched enough and if there is anything you can add to the research existing, or if you should choose a different topic.

Data Collection

After completion of the literature review and decision on the research method and design, you will create or use an existing data collection tool. Whether you use a design such as an interview, survey, or evaluate pre-existing data you will need to record your results. Data collection can be done through various tools. You will likely have a set timeframe in which you want to gather your data. The collection timeframe can vary depending upon the type of research being done. If you are gathering data from individuals, your tool or survey should provide information regarding the research, your contact information, and what to do should they no longer want their responses included in the research before completion. In addition, participants should be able to provide electronic or written signatures to give permission for the responses to be included in the research.

Chapter Two

DISSERTATION INTRODUCTION

There are numerous ways to gather your research data. You may even have pre-existing data available that you want to examine for patterns or comparisons. If you are gathering research data, you may use an existing tool with permission, or create your own survey or interview questionnaire. Data collection methods can also include tools such as recorded interviews for transcription, written surveys, electronic surveys, or focus groups. If your research is being performed at a business or employer, you will also need to get permission to conduct research at the facility. During your coursework, this information should be provided, and you will learn how to get the necessary permissions to complete your research study.

Presentation of Data

It is then time to review your results for responses and patterns. I found that the review and presentation of the data was one of the most exciting parts of the research study. At this point, you should be able to determine if you proved or disproved your initial hypothesis. There are different software and other tools available that can help you to review the data collected and observations. Once you have the results you will need to discuss and present them in your dissertation.

Chapter Two

DISSERTATION INTRODUCTION

The results discussion allows you to clearly express how the results compare to your hypothesis. In this section, you can explain any patterns or relationships found. You may want to discuss the problem that your research study was addressing. Furthermore, you can express thoughts on patterns related to specific groups, such as age ranges. The manner in which one variable can influence another variable can also be discussed. It is important to present your data clearly and in a format that can be easily understood. Each person who reads your research may have different education and topic familiarity levels. However, the research that you complete can create added value to the related stakeholders and the research community.

Chapter Two

DISSERTATION INTRODUCTION

Recommendations

Recommendations can also be made for the future. These thoughts could be related to employers, employees, or other stakeholder relationships. You may offer training ideas or activities or areas that should be examined. When making recommendations, it may be helpful to examine the literature review that you completed before starting your research study. This would allow you to see how your research fits in with prior studies. You should be able to make recommendations for parties involved in the topic of your research study.

Recommendations can also be made for future researchers. Your recommendations may include actions such as homing in on specific variables, looking at how a variable influences another, or completing a similar study for a different population or group of participants. You can discuss what you learned and observed from your research study. There may be areas that can be built upon or researched further. You can explain areas of growth or any additional research gaps that you have found.

Chapter Two

DISSERTATION INTRODUCTION

Oral Defense

The final portion of the dissertation process is the oral defense of your research. During this part, you will explain the factors such as the purpose, data collection, results, and recommendations of your research study. You will also answer any questions asked of you by the reviewers. I was extremely nervous about this portion of the process. I am not the best public speaker. I tend to speak faster than normal when I am nervous. However, the school did provide an oral defense presentation template and videos to review. This greatly helped with my preparation. I also recorded videos of myself performing mock oral defenses. I reviewed them to see what I could improve on. After your oral defense is deemed successful and passed, you will officially be a Dr. This was the best moment of my doctoral journey, next to being hooded at graduation.

3

THE Goals

Chapter Three

THE GOALS

One of the first actions that I would recommend would be to determine your reason for wanting to pursue a Doctorate. I would also suggest that this reason be written out and placed in an easily visible location. The use of a vision board was extremely helpful to me. It is important to know why you want to start the program. Thus, you will be able to continuously refer to this reason throughout your journey for motivation.

Skills

You may have short-term and long-term goals. One of the skills that can be strengthened through the completion of a doctoral program is public speaking. You may complete different projects and presentations during the program. The oral defense for the dissertation offers an opportunity for additional public speaking experience. This skill can also be beneficial for career activities, training, and presentations. Networking is also part of the doctoral program experience. During the journey, you will get to know other students and professors. You may also build relationships with members of organizations that you encounter during your research. These relationships may lead to continued growth and research beyond your dissertation.

Chapter Three
THE GOALS

Growth

One possible potential goal for obtaining a doctorate may be personal growth. The world is full of thoughts, ideas, and topics for study. Some individuals desire constant growth and gain satisfaction from achieving increasingly higher goals. If growth is one of your goals, it can be beneficial to write down some of your growth-related goals. These could be related to concepts such as desiring to learn more about a subject, reaching the highest level of education possible, or continuous learning. The completion of a doctorate program may grant you new perspectives on topics. You will also be able to share your learning with others.

Research

Another possible goal is to achieve research experience. The thought of performing research was somewhat intimidating for me initially. However, as I learned about different research methods, I became more comfortable with my research study. During the dissertation program, you will learn about different qualitative and quantitative research tools and designs. You may have never completed a research study. Or you may be an individual that enjoys performing research. Many students also perform additional research or publish in academic journals after completing the dissertation.

Chapter Three

THE GOALS

Career

    Career desires and goals may also influence a decision to pursue a doctorate. A significant amount of time during life is spent working. A doctorate degree may help you obtain additional career goals and growth. Doctorate degrees are offered in many different subjects. A doctorate may help you move up the career ladder. This can apply to jobs in the education field as well as other fields.

    You will learn in-depth information about your chosen topic. After completion, you will have the capability to explain the relationships involved and offer recommendations for solving a problem. In addition, you will add data to the research field. You will become a subject matter expert in your industry. The increase in education and doctorate achievement may allow you to get higher-level employment positions. Furthermore, the degree may assist you in obtaining teaching or other education positions.

DOCTORATE 101

4

THE Expectations

Chapter Four
THE EXPECTATIONS

As I progressed through my program, I learned that the road to completion was not straight. In addition, it often did not feel like I was making forward momentum. When I began my doctorate program, I assumed I would follow the steps and complete my program within a few years as expressed in my program timeline. It did not even cross my mind that the timeline could move. In hindsight, I was attempting to compare my doctoral program process to my prior undergraduate and graduate programs. However, the doctorate program and the process and requirements are significantly different and unique.

A year into my program my employer changed the requirements for tuition assistance. I was no longer qualified to receive help with tuition. This was a blow to my momentum and thoughts about my capability to finish in the program. In the end, I decided to try to continue in the program. I knew that my progress would be slower, as I would need to pay out of pocket for each course. However, I continued progressing.

The experience for each student is different. It is important to be cognizant of the fact that issues will arise as your life continues during your educational journey. As such, you may need to adjust your expectations periodically as you progress. Just remember that many other past or current students have also traveled this road. It is expected that unforeseen events and circumstances will be faced. You are not alone, and advancement is still possible if you desire to stay the course.

Chapter Four

THE EXPECTATIONS

Program Courses

The beginning of the doctorate program will likely consist of introduction courses followed by courses related to writing. The bulk will be subject matter courses related to your specific program. The dissertation process and qualitative or quantitative research classes will also be covered in program coursework. Each class will build up the foundation for the next class. I especially enjoyed the writing classes and the courses related to leadership and management.

During my program, I completed a single eight-week class at a time. Depending upon how long it has been since your last college course, it may take some time to get adjusted to the format of expected writing and assignments. My program was a mix of online courses and in-person learning. There are pros and cons to both methods. However, effective learning can occur in either environment. It will be important to ask questions to the instructor as needed and review all assignment feedback. In addition, don't be afraid to dialogue with your fellow student cohort and build relationships.

Chapter Four

THE EXPECTATIONS

Financing

A major influence on progress through a doctorate program is finances. The cost of a doctorate program can be expensive. I recommend looking into as many avenues of financial assistance as you can. Education loans are one option that numerous students use to further their education. Scholarships are offered by many schools and other organizations for a range of criteria, even at the doctoral level. Some schools also offer assistantships in which you work at some capacity at the school and your education costs are reduced.

Employer tuition assistance is an option I encourage everyone to inquire about. The only reason that I began my doctorate program when I did, was because my employer offered tuition assistance. This was greatly helpful for me. However, while I was progressing in my program, my employer changed the tuition assistance requirements for doctoral students. After the change, I no longer qualified for tuition assistance. Therefore, from that point on, I had to pay for my classes out of pocket. This was a blow to my progress. The need to pay for classes caused me to have to take more time off in between classes.

Chapter Four
THE EXPECTATIONS
Writing and Reading

Expectations also need to be created regarding your writing process. All writers are not the same. When I was completing my writing, I liked to set aside at least 2 to 3 hours on certain days to write. Other people may try to write as little as 30 minutes to an hour a day. The daily writing method was not the best method for my mind. When ideas come to me, I like to focus and write for a few hours and get as much written as I can. However, each person has a different schedule, focus, and best-fitting writing practice. So, I encourage you to try different writing schedules and find the writing method that best works for your life, schedule, and writing style. Whatever you decide, be sure to keep writing regularly.

The writing style for doctorate programs may also be different from prior education writing style and expectations. During your classes, you may get feedback on the writing aspect. It can take time to adjust to the requirements. There will also be specific formatting needed for your dissertation. Books or other documents should be provided in your classes to assist you. Writing is a valuable form of expression. Use all the tools available to you to create your best writing and maintain momentum. Save your writing work regularly and in different places.

Chapter Four
THE EXPECTATIONS

During the doctorate program, you will read a large number of articles and books. These may include hard copies as well as online versions. There will be required readings for classes and then there will be those that you desire to read on your own to assist with understanding different components of the dissertation process or for your dissertation literature review. Be patient with yourself. As it can seem daunting or overwhelming to read so much. It is common to reread information and bookmark sections or pages for later reference. Take your time. Use your classmate and instructor network to discuss things when needed for better understanding.

Chapter Four

THE EXPECTATIONS

Feedback

You will learn the importance and frequency of the receipt of feedback upon entering your first course. As you progress you will get more comfortable. During the dissertation work, you will get a large amount of written and verbal feedback over time. You will have multiple revisions to your dissertation before the final result. You will get feedback from course instructors as well as your committee. At times it can be discouraging to see so many items that need to be reviewed and corrected. It is easy to become overwhelmed. I recommend that you set a deadline for when you want to have all of the corrections completed. Afterwards you can focus on one correction at a time. Eventually, you will complete all necessary edits and will continue to move forward.

Chapter Four

THE EXPECTATIONS

All But Dissertation (ABD)

There will come a point in your program when you will be abd status. This status is what doctoral students refer to as all but dissertation. This is when you have completed all of your subject matter core courses of the program and finally only have the dissertation left to complete. Students stay in abd status for various amounts of time. The length of time in this status is influenced by factors such as finances, research permissions, revision feedback, and other life experiences. When I began my doctoral program one of my professors expressed during a class discussion that not all of the students starting the program would end up completing the program. Some students obtained their doctorate before I did. Others finished the program after I did. While some students did not complete the program. It is also okay to take breaks. There are also instances where doctoral students take breaks for months or even years and then return to the doctorate program and successfully finish. In the end, you must do what is best for you.

5

POSITIVE *Focus*

Chapter Five

POSITIVE FOCUS

Throughout the doctoral program, it will be necessary to stay motivated and maintain a positive outlook. Positive focus and thoughts can help to carry you through some of the stressful and tiring times. It can also be a benefit to surround yourself with positive energy and people who pour love and encouragement into you. It is expected to encounter setbacks and to feel disappointment from them. However, in order to get to the end goal, you must keep moving forward.

Competition

At the end of the day, you have to run your own race. It is sometimes easy to compare our own journeys and experiences to those of others. The doctoral program you choose will have a course timeline and tentative completion expectations. For example, my program listed timeline was 3 years. There will be students that you start the program with that may complete the doctoral program before you and after you. That is okay. It is in those types of moments that you must focus on why you started and the progress you have made. The focus should stay on your goals and journey. A saying that I consistently say to myself is that I am my own competition.

Chapter Five

POSITIVE FOCUS

Flexible Timeline

It is common to face many issues such as financial setbacks, the need for a mental break, health issues, family issues, or even education issues. During my journey, I endured changes to my committee chair and other committee members. Financial costs also affected my ability to take courses. In addition, after review of my proposal and dissertation, I faced numerous reviews and revision requests before I finally completed the program. I found that it was a good idea to remember that my completion timeline was tentative. I wrote out a timeline for completing tasks. I made adjustments as necessary.

During this process, you may also feel less connected to friends and family due to the amount of time and dedication required for classes, assignments, and working on the dissertation. You will need to find a balance between keeping educational momentum and not losing total social touch and interaction with family and friends. Find what best works for you. The amount of time you are able to focus and work on the dissertation and assignments can also affect your timeline. There will be things within and without of your control that will impact the length of time it takes for you to obtain your doctorate. Focus on what you can control.

Chapter Five
POSITIVE FOCUS
Accountability

Self-awareness can be a valuable quality as you move toward completing your doctorate. Only you are aware of your true capability and the level of effort you are willing to use to try to complete your doctoral goals. Accountability is an important element of progression. The ability to complete assignments and set timelines for corrections and writing can assist you in maintaining accountability. I encourage you to be intentional with your time and your effort.

A second source important for accountability is family and friends. Some individuals may have larger or smaller friend and family groups. However, all levels of support can be beneficial. Some individuals are able to easily exhibit self-accountability. However, in life in general I have personally found that in some circumstances I perform better when I have an accountability partner. It is up to you to decide what environment best helps to successfully hold yourself accountable and complete goals. Family both immediate and outside of your household can help support you through communication and listening as you share your experiences and ask for advice. Your friends can also offer support as you work on your dissertation and try to stay motivated. You may have friends that you have known for years or newer friends. You may also likely make friends from school as you move through the doctorate program.

Chapter Five
POSITIVE FOCUS

    The chair and committee members for your dissertation can also support your accountability efforts. There will be set expectations you have for your committee and your committee will also have expectations of you. These are normally discussed when the committee is formed. The regular communication and discussions along with timely revisions and feedback will also support your accountability.

    No one will understand your doctoral journey as well as fellow doctoral students and those individuals who have completed a doctorate program. I highly suggest that you take advantage of your program student cohort and exchange contact information. The student network that you create can help you gain numerous accountability partners. In addition, you can vent and share experiences with other students who can relate to you. Furthermore, you will also be able to observe the progress of other students. When other students graduate, you may be further encouraged that it is possible to continue toward the goal and obtain your doctorate degree.

Chapter Five
POSITIVE FOCUS

Motivation

 The completion of a doctorate is not an experience that many people can relate to. There were many days of tears and mental exhaustion during my journey. I had discussions with family, friends, and my committee along the way. I believe that it was helpful to keep in touch with fellow students pursuing their doctorate degree. We were able to understand and motivate each other when needed. Sometimes you will have to encourage and motivate yourself. You have to do the work and others may not always understand your thoughts and feelings.

 Motivation is a factor that will be important to focus on throughout doctoral coursework. Life goes on as you progress through the program. Not only your life but the lives of the friends and family around you. It can be frustrating to try to juggle coursework and time with family friends or for work responsibilities. There will be times when you will miss fun activities or no longer spend time doing things that you are used to doing. Your loved ones may also have difficulty accepting when you are not able to attend some events. But try to keep your goal in mind and stay motivated. There will be a point when you will have your free time again.

Chapter Five
POSITIVE FOCUS

Motivation levels will fluctuate over time. There will always be a need to try to engage self-motivation. It may be helpful to figure out what tools or activities best help you maintain steady motivation. During my doctorate degree journey, there were several points in time when I considered stopping and wondered if I would ever complete the program. At the core, I knew that I was capable of completing the program. This thought kept me moving forward, even if the steps were small. I also practiced celebrating small victories along the way.

DOCTORATE 101

6

FIVE Lessons Learned

Chapter Six
FIVE LESSONS LEARNED

    I learned so much about myself and my capabilities during my doctoral journey. There are some things that I wish I would have been aware of before I started my program. I am sharing a few of those thoughts in hopes that they may help others better prepare mentally and emotionally for the pursuit of a doctorate degree.

1. Run your own race.

    The beginning of a doctorate program will consist of courses related to your area of study, such as management, information technology, education, etc. Once you have completed the program's main subject courses, you will move on to the dissertation-focused courses and work. The dissertation is a large research project to take on. It can become overwhelming. As I attended classes I connected with students. There are some students that I exchanged contact information with and kept in touch with as we moved through classes. We checked in on each other and congratulated each other when degrees were attained. I have often heard individuals say that comparison is the thief of joy. Sometimes it can be disheartening when you see other students completing the program or progressing faster. However, everyone's path is different. When I look back at my first draft compared to my final approved dissertation, the growth is evident. I encourage you to stay focused on your work and progress.

Chapter Six

FIVE LESSONS LEARNED

2. The program completion date can be a moving target.

     My Doctor of Management program course timeline was listed as 3 years. I consider myself an organized person. I like calendars, reminders, setting deadlines, and marking off progress. I used these tools often during my courses. After the completion of my core courses such as business and leadership courses and quantitative and qualitative research courses, there was a point where all that remained was dissertation coursework. It was at this juncture that I realized that my anticipated graduation date was tentative. I continued to be informed that revisions were needed before moving further to collect data. As a result, I had to request an extension in the program. Consequently, my anticipated graduation date was pushed further into the future. I did not complete the program as early as I anticipated. However, I did graduate.

Chapter Six

FIVE LESSONS LEARNED

3. Expect challenges and setbacks.

When I started my doctoral program, I did not think about the challenges that I could face. There is a range of hindrances and setbacks that doctoral students may encounter. There are health-related situations that may arise for you or your family that can affect your ability to attend classes. The possibility also exists that changes may occur regarding your chair and committee members. For example, during my program, I had to change my chair once and had to find replacement committee members twice. In addition, financial factors can create challenges to progress. The need to pay for some courses out of pocket can have an impact on when classes can be scheduled. You may not be able to anticipate all of the challenges that you may face. However, just knowing that facing setbacks is a possibility may help you respond positively and timely to your future challenges.

Chapter Six
FIVE LESSONS LEARNED

4. Support and breaks are a necessity.

    During the doctorate program, you will do a significant amount of reading and writing. Your writing will be reviewed. In addition, you will receive large amounts of feedback, which will require revisions. It is important to focus on your work and goals, while timely responding to feedback. However, it is also necessary to make time for breaks. The doctoral program journey can be stressful. I encourage you to make time for regular stress relief activities.

You may also find support from loved ones as well as current or past doctoral students. The practice of venting and discussing ideas and experiences with doctoral students can offer help regarding how to deal with various situations. Family and friends can also listen to your concerns and participate in activities that you enjoy. The uses of breaks and support are just as important as your writing schedule. Progress requires both work and rest.

Chapter Six

FIVE LESSONS LEARNED

5. Program completion is possible.

    The road to graduation may be full of surprises and curves. However, the joy felt upon completion is immense. While working toward your doctorate degree you may hear instructors or doctoral graduates say that the best dissertation is a done dissertation. I believe that this statement serves to encourage doctoral students, not to overcomplicate their dissertation. Find the clear focus of your research and execute the data collection and results analysis. Keep moving forward.

DOCTORATE 101

7

THE
Reward

Chapter Seven
THE REWARD

In the end, obtaining my doctorate is one of my proudest accomplishments. I am the first person in my immediate family to complete a doctorate. The feeling when I walked into the graduation arena to my seat is indescribable. I have never been full of such joy and fulfillment. My research allowed me to offer solutions to a problem and provide insight into the research field. It also offered possible opportunities for future research and professional endeavors.

The reward for each individual person will no doubt be different. However, no matter the path, hindrances, or length of time, there will be a reward. I am hopeful that you will find your rewards valuable and worth the time and experiences of your journey. Once you get to the reward stage, all of the past tears, stress, frustration, and sleepless nights are no longer a focus.

Professional

A doctorate degree can lead to a professional reward for many people. During the doctorate program, you will learn in-depth information about your chosen field. This could be an area such as information technology, business management, nursing, or other fields. This high level of study can be applied in the work field. It can also be used to perform additional related research. You may be able to apply to higher-level positions with more growth opportunities or increased salary potential.

Chapter Seven
THE REWARD

Some doctoral students may expect immediate upward movement after obtaining their doctorate. This is not always the case. It can take time for the opportunity to move up professionally. It can be very beneficial to have a doctorate degree. However, along with the degree, it is also important to communicate your knowledge, skills, and strengths to current or potential employers and put the qualities to practical use in your job.

Chapter Seven

THE REWARD

Educational

Rewards can also be related to education. Doctoral students who have teaching positions or other positions at an educational institution may also desire to move up. For example, an individual who teaches high school or undergraduate college students may want to move up to teach doctoral students. In addition, a doctoral graduate of any career field may also want to do some part-time teaching at the doctoral level. As time progresses new goals could be found or created. It could also become a goal to later mentor doctoral students or become a doctoral student's chair at a university doctoral program. While many doctoral programs have committee chairs and committee members that are instructors of the university in which the doctoral student is enrolled, some programs may allow for a doctorate-educated committee member that is not a university instructor.

Chapter Seven
THE REWARD

Personal

    A personal goal is one that is important and valuable to you. Other people may not understand your goal, vision, or reason for pursuing a higher-level education. However, the attainment of a doctorate degree takes you on a journey that only fellow doctoral learners can comprehend. It can be helpful to remember your personal goals and track your accomplishments. Since the completion of my dissertation, my research study has been cited in additional research literature. This provided an unforeseen level of fulfillment. It was wonderful to see that what I added to the research world has been built upon and progressed by another researcher.

8

FINAL Thoughts

Chapter Eight
FINAL THOUGHTS

I have received numerous rewards from obtaining my doctorate degree. I had some complications along the way. But I am extremely glad that I kept going and completed my goal. Thank you for taking the time to read this book. My hope is that this short guide offers some program and experience insight that helps introduce you to the doctoral experience and motivates you as you progress toward your doctorate degree. May this book be a verbal cheerleader when you need one. I also encourage you to read additional books concerning the dissertation and doctoral experience that go more in-depth and give more comprehensive information.

I am Dr. Dawn McLucas. I began my doctorate program in 2009. I completed the program in 2018. If I was able to finish, there is hope for you too. Find your support system. Celebrate small victories. Remember why you started. If you would like additional doctoral information and support, please visit my website at blueprintambitions.com to learn about the Doctorate 101 digital online course which will provide expanded comprehensive guidance and information. There will also be opportunities for one-on-one support sessions. The next course is starting soon. Best wishes on getting your doctorate.

HELPFUL REFERENCES

RESOURCE 1

Dissertations and Theses From Start to Finish by John D. Cone and Sharon Foster

RESOURCE 2

Publication Manual of the American Psychological Association

RESOURCE 3

Qualitative Research from Start to Finish by Robert K. Yin

RESOURCE 4

Quantitative Research Methods for Professionals by W. Paul Vogt

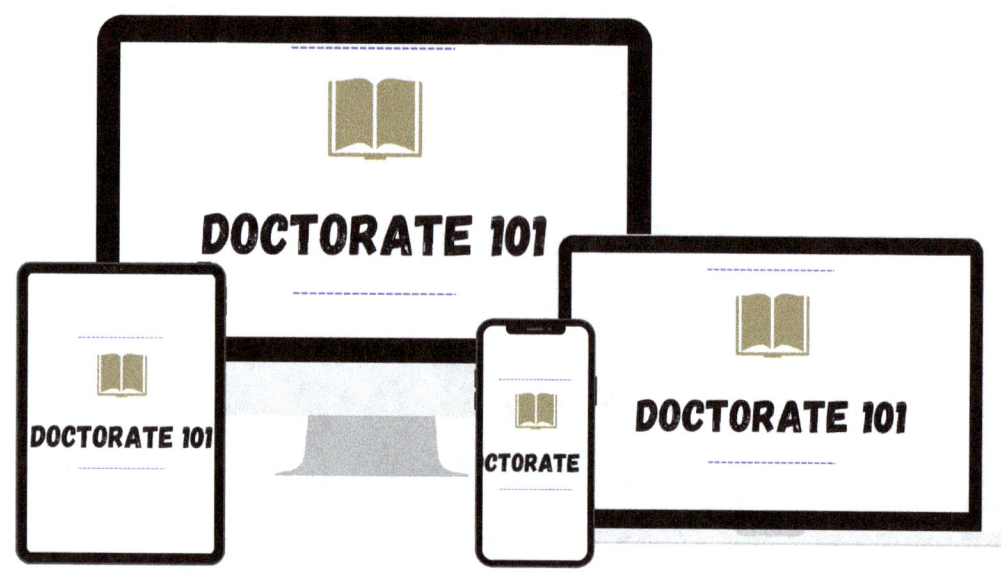

GET THE FULL DOCTORATE 101 COURSE!

ARE YOU EXPERIENCING ANXIOUSNESS ABOUT THE START OF YOUR DOCTORAL PROGRAM?

HAVE YOU STARTED TO FEEL OVERWHELMED DURING YOUR FIRST DOCTORAL PROGRAM COURSES?

IF SO, THEN THIS COURSE IS FOR YOU. LET'S WORK ON EASING YOUR ANXIETY AND LEARNING SOME FOUNDATIONAL CONCEPTS TO HELP MAINTAIN MOMENTUM TOWARD YOUR GOAL.

The self-paced online class provides doctoral students with an introduction, preparation, information, insights, and materials to confidently start a doctorate program. Visit blueprintambitions.com for more information.

Doctorate 101

OUR SERVICES

DOCTORATE 101
HOW TO SURVIVE AND THRIVE

$49

The online course is comprised of lectures, information, exercises and tips to provide students a helpful foundation regarding the start of a doctorate program. The goal is to offer students motivation, relevant information and assistance as they progress through the doctorate program.

DOCTORATE 101 COACHING

$50

One-on-one coaching sessions: In these sessions, the coach assists the doctoral student with individual questions presented as they progress through the program.

CHOOSING A DISSERTATION TOPIC

FREE

This is a FREE digital book with information in it to assist students with choosing a dissertation topic.

blueprintambitions.com

OUR BOOKS

DOCTORATE 101 $7.99

A concise guidebook full of resources, tips, experiences, and tools to assist prospective and new doctoral students on their journey.

THE DISSERTATION PLANNER $6.99

This 100-page dissertation planner includes problem and purpose creation techniques, topic choosing methods, literature review concepts, milestone tools, and plenty of lined pages for notes and more.

DISSERTATION JOUNRAL $6.99

This 100-page journal serves as a tool to allow your thoughts to be captured and organized.

blueprintambtions.com

"TO LEARN, IS TO GROW. THE VALUE OF AN EDUCATION IS LIMITLESS."

— Dr. Dawn McLucas
DOCTORATE 101

NOTES

NOTES

DOCTORATE 101

BY DR. DAWN MCLUCAS

Let's Stay in Touch

 BLUEPRINTAMBITIONSLLC@GMAIL.COM

 BLUEPRINTAMBITIONS.COM

 @BLUEPRINT_AMBITIONS

 FACEBOOK.COM/DOCDNM

www.ingramcontent.com/pod-product-compliance
Lightning Source LLC
Chambersburg PA
CBHW050323010526
44119CB00003B/84